Life according to Maude

Other Books by John Lund

Animal Antics
Animal Wisdom

By John Lund, Creator of *Animal Antics*

Written by Peter Stein

Andrews McMeel
Publishing

Kansas City

Life according to *Maude*

05 06 07 08 09 WKT 10 9 8 7 6 5 4 3 2 1

ISBN: 0-7407-5142-5
Library of Congress Control Number: 200411400

Art Direction: Collette Carter
Design and Production: Heather Stewart Design

Introduction

Day in, day out, we all have our triumphs and our frustrations, our must-haves and our "eeewwws!" How many of us come right out and say exactly what we think and feel about this quirky predicament called life? Well, not to worry. Maude is here to do just that—for all of us.

Ever feel like telling the world exactly what you think about relationships (you're always right), dieting (it's mostly wrong), and shoe sales (in a word, "yes")? Maude will. She has a unique way of getting right to the heart of the matter—and then telling it like it is, shooting straight from the (furry) hip. Her sense of style and attitude make her a pure original. Her sense of humor makes this cat very human indeed.

A fashion maven, great girlfriend, habitual shopper, unabashed gossip, life-loving, diet-hating, salon-going, feline diva, Maude imparts priceless bits of saucy wisdom—perfect for laughing, sharing, and patterning your entire life after. Maude would have it no other way.

True happiness is found within. Within salons, pastry shops, and boutiques, that is.

Pampering is not a choice.
It is a religion.

It may be true that love
is all you need . . .

but sometimes chocolate
is all you *want*.

Exercise daily . . .
your right to indulge!

It's not true that beauty
is only skin deep.

It's makeup deep
and clothes deep, too.

The best things in life are free.
Or on sale!

Meditation clears the mind.
And you'll be a more
effective shopper
with a clear mind.

Good friends
are nature's way of saying,
"Cocktails, anyone?"

I'm never lonely—
those few extra pounds
always keep me company.

Remember,
gossip is a terrible thing.

(But only if you're not in the room.)

When life gets stressful,
nothing can soothe the soul
like the great indoors.

The only way to dream big dreams is to nap big naps.

Home is where the heart is.
But the mall is where the soul is.

Never let life's responsibilities interfere with pampering.

Three simple words to true happiness: bitch, bitch, bitch.

Spend a little time every day doing what comes naturally.

Shopping!

Sometimes when I'm desperate,
I look to my Higher Power.
And then I realize, nope,
no chocolate there, either.

Live today . . .
for we may diet tomorrow!

Never let other people's jealousy
rob you of feeling good
about being superior to them.

Follow your bliss.

If it leads to cocktails, so be it.

Beware of PMS—
Post Munchies Syndrome.

Money can't buy happiness.
But it can buy lots of shoes,
which are even better than happiness.

Relationships are a two-way street.

My way and the wrong way!

Sometimes you have to accept
life's little disappointments—

like when you get to the salon and
you realize you're already perfect.

Men. You can't live *with* them, you can't live *with* them.

Always take time to stop and smell the shoe sales!

Tell yourself
how beautiful you are every day.
They don't call it a vanity for nothing.

It's smart to follow your heart.
But it's *fun* to follow your taste buds!

Aren't men wonderful?
They make it so *easy*
to see how superior we are.

"Sexy" is a state of mind.
No matter *what* state your body is in.

Shopping is an extreme sport.
Be a champion.

Live your life and forget your age.

(The good news is, the longer you
live, the more you'll forget!)

I was following a diet closely...
but it ducked into a corner
and got away.

I say, shop till you drop . . .
a paycheck or two!

Celebrate life every day...
but save some energy for the nights!

Take a little time every day
to reflect...
on how gorgeous you are!

Sometimes it's important
to sit down and acknowledge
that life is, indeed, sweet.

Special Thanks

to Collette Carter and Peter Stein
for their creativity and enthusiasm.

And to Bow Wow Productions
for Maude and her friends.